Val
m[illegible]
Bu[illegible]
Penny.

How to Read Character in Handwriting

HOW TO READ CHARACTER IN *Handwriting*

COMPILED BY
JULIE HINTON

Copper Beech Publishing

Published in Great Britain 1995 by
Copper Beech Publishing Ltd

ISBN 1-898617-10-4

Compiled by Julie Hinton
Editor Jan Barnes

A CIP catalogue record for this book is available from the British Library.

Copper Beech Publishing Ltd
P O Box 159 East Grinstead
Sussex RH19 4FS England

Late Victorian England was a time when several books were published offering readers a way to read character in handwriting. This little book is based on one of the most popular examples published in 1890. Julie Hinton has looked back at Victorian graphology and found it to be remarkably like the handwriting analysis she practises today.

INTRODUCTION

We were all taught to write in the same way but each of our handwritings is unique.

Our individual character and what is happening to us at the time, will show in our handwriting. We are what we write!

Graphologists do not claim to tell a person's history from their handwriting, nor can they foresee the future.

However, handwriting can reveal our strengths and weaknesses, our potential - whether we are adventurous, energetic, modest or romantic - or a combination of them all.

Graphology has remained almost unchanged for more than 100 years.

Enjoy discovering character traits using this little book. Any handwriting that now comes your way will have new meaning ..!

Julie Hinton

GLOSSARY

Angular style

Arcade style

Garland style

Thread style

For more information about these four styles turn to page 97.

Flying letters

Knotted letters

Starting strokes

Hooks

GLOSSARY

Zones: every example of handwriting can be divided into three zones:

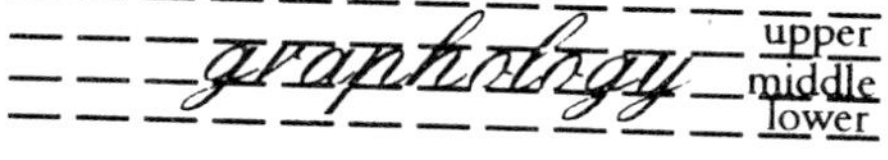

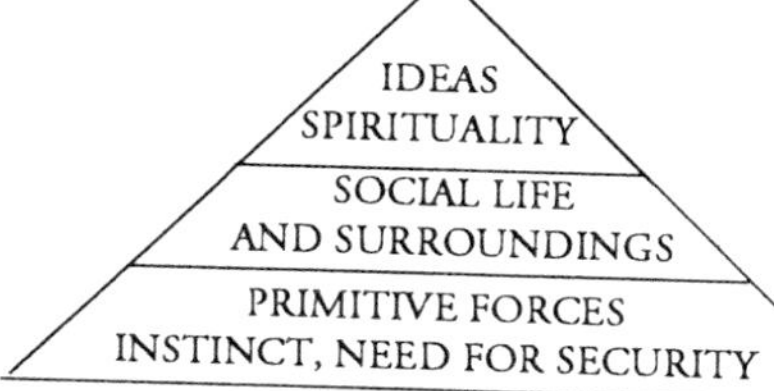

CHARACTERISTICS APPARENT IN HANDWRITING

All, or nearly all of the passions, affections and weaknesses of human nature may be discovered from the handwriting. This may appear a very bold statement to advance; but I venture to say, that before this book is ended the assertion will have been justified.

ADVENTUROUS A determined right slant is the best indicator of an adventurous character. The layout on the page will be your next clue; showing a wide left margin and a non existent right. This is an indication of people who are always looking forward, rather than living in the past. The writing will be large and unrestricted. *(page 12)*

AFFECTION can be determined almost at a glance in any handwriting. Its best characteristics are long loops to the letters, with a rather sloping hand. The letters are tenderly formed, if one may so speak; and the y frequently turns back instead of rounding to the left. Frequently, rounded letters will be seen, in a rather upright hand. This is a modification of affection; a somewhat harder and most selfish type. Again, when the writing is thick, rounded, and sloping to the right, and also embellished with long loops, there is passionate affection and a regard for the opposite sex. *(page 12)*

AMBITION is ascertainable from an energetic, angular and upward sloping handwriting, combined with quite a

Thanks for lots

Determined right slant
(Adventurous)

looked really write this

Long loops and a sloping hand
(Affection)

firm pressure. The individual words will rise. Another good indicator is large capitals in the signature. *(page 14)*

ANGER will be found in quick movements of the pen. If the t is barred high, and in a 'fly-away' manner, particularly when the bar is firm and thick, you may be certain that the writer is a touchy, irritable person. A quick-tempered person will frequently have long angular starting strokes to their initial letters.

ARDOUR is represented in graphology in much the same manner as energy. Ardour will be visible in elongated capitals, and the firm sweep of the letters; in long flying bars to t and the general 'go' in the writing. *(page 14)*

bike and ride us
about five miles
had a punchure

Energetic upward sloping writing
(Ambition)

best boon, this sa
who loves thee be
es that I bear to
unaptly told

Long flying t-bars
(Ardour)

but I do tend
to go in too many
directions at once
Angela M. Morgan

Clear graceful capitals
(Artistic)

ARTISTIC TASTE is a rather more complex characteristic allied to poetic feeling and refinement. This will be found in the clearness and the gracefulness of the capitals. People who have a taste for sculpture and love for architecture generally make their capitals of a print-like accuracy, without necessarily the same signs of imagination as the painter. Artistic taste is also indicated by a person who leaves a "frame" of paper around the writing. *(page 15)*

BASHFULNESS is a combination of shyness and modesty. Look for close fitting strokes of capital letters, and small letters which are even, moderate, and not showy. A leftward leaning writing can indicate bashfulness and moderation in taste and habits.

People of great self-assertion, will write a big showy hand, and space out the capitals. Your modest and retiring correspondent, on the contrary, will be modest and self-contained, and this will be evident in the writing! *(page 18)*

BENEVOLENCE is discovered in the character by the openness and clearness of the writing: there is no violence in it; but there is activity displayed, with clear candid letters, and a truthful, open nature. Indications of a benevolent

Labour with what zeal we
Something still remains
Something uncompleted
Waits the rising of the

Close fitting strokes of capital letters
(Bashfulness)

CROSS-COUNTRY Which

one week. Its like a clear
smarter Venice with lace

Cautious well punctuated hand
(Business)

person are large, even writing, flowing and graceful, with endings to the letters which slope to the right.

BUSINESS habits are generally recognised by a neat, cautious, well-punctuated writing, in which abbreviations sometimes occur. A methodical writing, an orderliness, is observable throughout, and the stops carefully inserted, the i carefully dotted, and the t carefully crossed. More energy, will and dash in the script, will be observable in the writing of those who decide rapidly in business matters.*(page 18)*

CALMNESS is perceptible in even sizes of letters; if they were of different sizes versatility would be indicated, or restlessness. Upright writing, with a

Thanks for
thoughtful touch
I'm afraid I

Upright with a round appearance
(Calmness)

much since then.
The Christmas time
was lovely to see

Small tightly formed letters
(Caution)

round appearance to it is a good indicator of someone with this disposition. *(page 20)*

CANDOUR can be seen in widely spaced lines and rightward sloping letters. Also, if the words are separated evenly, there is no mistake possible.

CAUTION can be discerned by small, tightly formed letters. These people need time to prepare - and begin words with small starting strokes. There is also a tendency to put in the stops after numbers and signatures. *(page 20)*

COLDNESS is seen in the handwriting of selfish people. These people write upright hands, without generous flowing curves and capitals. The letters are

I will

account

Thin upright without curves
(Coldness)

The Scottish

time of

Pyramid shapes to the top of m and n
(Criticism)

generally closed up, showing them to be self-contained; and if the writing be rather thin, there is little love wasted on any one! There is no rightward sloping tenderness and no long lower loops - the writing is also generally small.
(*page 22*)

CONSCIENTIOUS people write steady, even hands, with a firm decided pen. Clear space between lines shows a sense of justice and neatness. A conscientious writer generally writes in an unhurried fashion.

CRITICISM is shown by small, angular handwriting, pyramid shapes to the top of the letter m and n, denoting a sharp perceptive mind. (*page 22*)

Thread-like writing.
(Deceit)

that go with the time
seeing all of you
She had met Louisa

Every dot and dash carefully inserted
(Detail)

CULTIVATION is evidenced by rather small writing. Some letters, especially the small d, will be looped, and sometimes united with the succeeding letters without the pen leaving the page. These are all signs of literary tastes - that is, a taste for writing and literary work.

DECEIT can be thought of as concealment of the facts! In this thread-like writing there is a desire to conceal the letters, to run them into indistinguishable lines and signs by which the sense can only be guessed at, not clearly deduced. The lines are uneven, the letters are confused, 'of no size in particular', and the writer will often end his words with a mere line! *(page 24)*

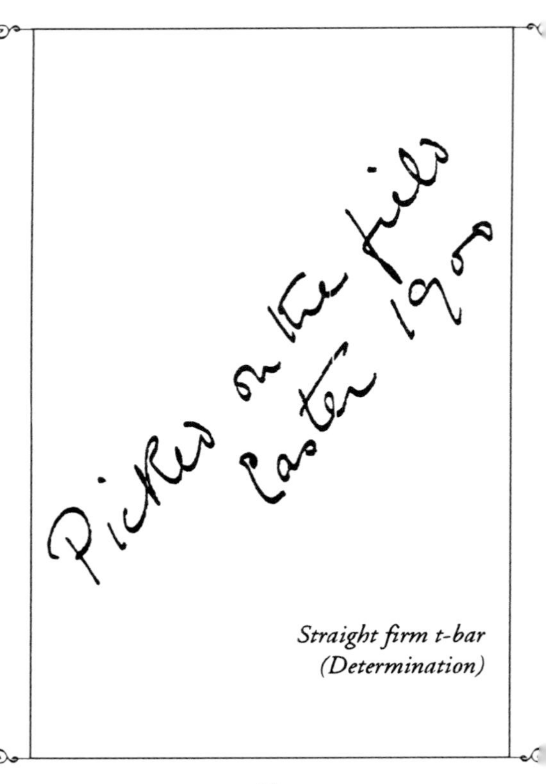

Straight firm t-bar
(Determination)

DESPONDENCY is one of the most easily recognised traits in graphology. A weak desponding person, or one in ill-health, who is temporarily out of spirits and therefore lacking in energy, will permit the hand to fall. As a result, the writing will slope downwards.

DETAIL displays itself in small neat writing, in which every dot and dash is carefully inserted and the writing is frequently upright. There does not appear to be much energy in such writing; the mind is too careful to run riot! This writing is almost always simple and legible, without unnecessary ornament. *(page 24)*

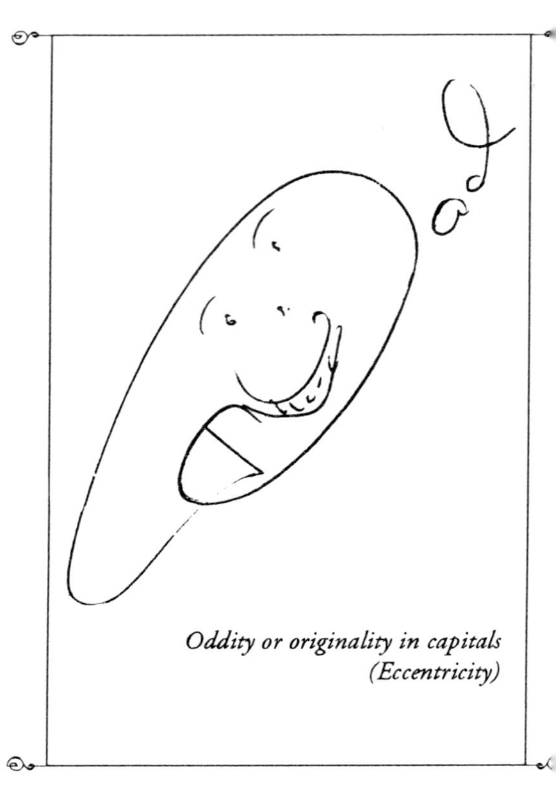

Oddity or originality in capitals (Eccentricity)

DETERMINATION can readily be recognised by the firmness of the writing, and the steady crossing of the t. A straight firm bar to every small t will indicate to us that the writer is determined. If the bar is rather 'fly away' they have energy and a quick temper as well! *(page 26)*

DIPLOMACY Seldom does an individual of very diplomatic mind write distinctly - they conceal their thoughts, having cultivated the habit of concealment. Diplomacy may be illustrated by an undulating and wary manner of writing, distinct enough, no doubt, but the tendency to conceal is there. Frequently writers of vivid imagination are difficult to decipher, but this obscurity of writing is evidence of haste, not

the half, at any rate.

courage! – see, here are

'twill soon be finished.

Carefulness of ink and space
(Economy)

Caught his

the room

T crossed high over following letters
(Energy)

of deceit. The letters are generally all there, but not carefully formed. The hand endeavours to overtake the imagination, and an indistinct writing is the result!

ECCENTRICITY Some oddity or originality will be very evident in the script! An out of the way form of writing their capital letters and unrestricted style will be found in the writing of all eccentric people. Very often these indications will be found in the writings of highly imaginative and clever people who have deviated much from the way they were originally taught to write. *(page 28)*

ECONOMY The signs of this virtue are evident - a carefulness of ink and space. We frequently see handwriting in which economy seems allied with a wish for display - a spacing out of lines. Circumstances and necessity can compel economy where the natural bent of the mind is to spend money. The letters will be clear and distinct; with no waste, nor disorder; though the writing may be hasty, there is no swagger - the lines are rigidly honest. *(page 30)*

Consider the difference between the above and Extravagance on page 39.

EGOTISM is seen in large initial capitals and a pronounced signature in comparison to the rest of the writing. If there is also a full middle zone, you can be sure the person will demand attention!

We wandered
The children
At the gate
Mark is so
on animals –
he just adores
them!!

Upward slope, full zones
(Enthusiasm)

—Thanks for

thick to them

the autograph—

T-bar crossed hastily upwards
(Excitability)

ELOQUENCE If the writing displays a logical sequence of ideas in the flow of words and letters, we may say that the person has the gift of speaking. Talent will be seen in the curving small d, which is united with the subsequent letter in many instances. Consider also clearness of handwriting, the joining of letters and a rightward slant.

ENERGY The writing is firm, rather angular and often ascending; the t will be crossed high up, sometimes over the following letters. This rather lengthened stroke also indicates perseverance. There is firmness perceptible, no softness or laziness. You may also find the high loops of enthusiasm, but the latter is the fringe, whereas the energy is the substance! *(page 30)*

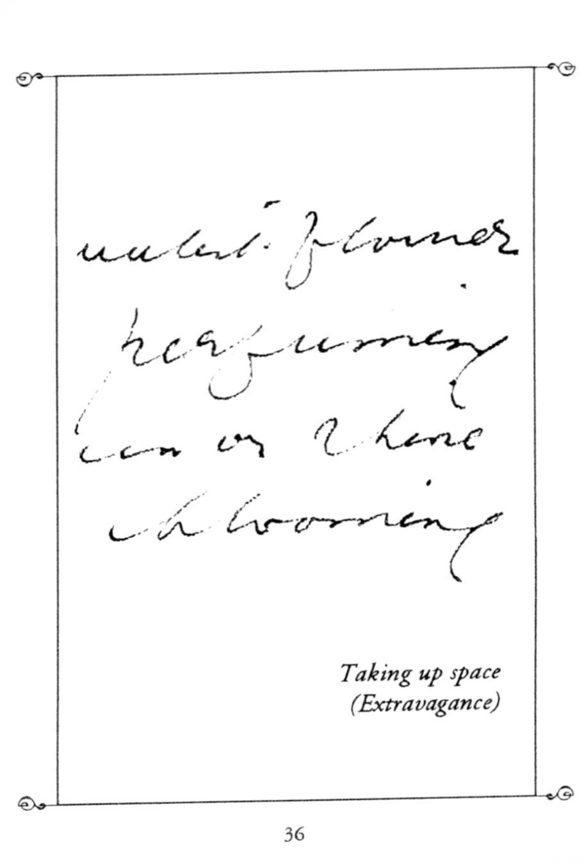

Taking up space
(Extravagance)

ENTHUSIASM is similar to vivacity. Look for a strong, positive handwriting with an upward slope, with a balance between the zones which are full. T bars and i dots are written with exuberance and are therefore dashed to the right. This writing calls to be noticed! *(page 33)*

EXCITABILITY can be deduced by the hurried style of the writing. The letters are uneven. The t-bar is generally crossed hastily upwards and high; and the writing is frequently thick and very decided. It may also slope, in which case you will expect tenderness and kindness, but also capability for 'tempers' when the occasion offers. Reason writes clearly and evenly so; on the contrary, an excitable person will dash

a link from
which made them
the present &
their future.

Clear, plain equal letters
(Frankness)

off correspondence and even in calmer moments will be betrayed by their innate excitability! *(page 34)*

EXTRAVAGANCE An extravagant person will take up space; having grand ideas, so the writer will sprawl in a somewhat careless way over the paper, write probably a large hand and omit cautious dots and dashes. When the indications of 'self' (capital I, large expansive signature) are visible in a somewhat generous writing, we may premise that the individual is generous in cases where their own enjoyment is concerned. *(page 36)*

FALSEHOOD is shown in writing by indistinct and wavy lines, threads of ink doing duty for a succession of letters!

who then
minutes later
"sorry dear

Curling final strokes
(Generosity)

My name is
thirty one
west Sussex

Well rounded curves
(Gentleness)

People who write like this are often rather evasive in manner, and are not always to be trusted to keep their word!

FINESSE is visible in the majority of handwritings: it is sometimes very strongly accentuated, sometimes faintly, as 'tact', sometimes the writing is extremely 'diplomatic'. Words are smaller at the end than at the beginning, the letters dwindle away. This reveals a tendency is 'throw dust in people's eyes', but such people do not deceive you.

FRANKNESS is revealed by clearness and honesty of purpose in distinct and even writing, well-formed letters and open words. The letters will be of the same elevation in the words, which do

A vulgar flourish
(Grandeur)

Today he saw the sea for
at which he just stared.
started to walk. In the

Uniform size with equal spacing
(Honesty)

not terminate in sharp points, but rather in rounded curves. Clear, plain, equal letters of sustained size are the principal signs. *(page 38)*

FRIENDLINESS can be seen at a glance. Garland style predominates with a definite forward slant - revealing an outward personality with an interest in others. The writing will have a harmonious, rhythmic appearance and will be medium to large in size. Look for small gaps between words - this is a reliable sign that the writer seeks company!

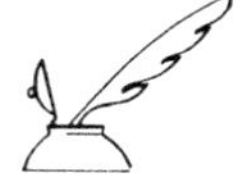

My dear Louisa

Large elegant capitals
(Imaginative)

desperate men are !!!

Flying t-bars
(Impulsiveness)

GENEROSITY, there is a generosity of the mind as well as of the hand. The garland style writing will be open, rounded and have curling finals: the letters m and n will be written in the shape of a u, in good-natured fashion. Clearness and open-handed writing are the characteristics to look for; the writer will be benevolent, but not without caution. *(page 40)*

GENTLENESS is a character trait which is easily recognised. Look for well-rounded curves and a clear, unhurried layout on the paper . There is no real want of will, however there is firmness enough, but with a rounded softness of character. *(page 40)*

I. should have

Rounded turns to the letters
(Indolence)

working
from

Kate

Knotted t
(Jealousy)

GRANDEUR is visible in masterly large letters. There is always a certain amount of pretension in such writing, and if the mind is vulgar, there will frequently be seen a vulgar flourish!
(page 42)

HONESTY is shown by clear writing, equal spaces between words and lines and overall even handwriting. This writing will not show the characteristics of artistic writing, but will be of uniform size, together with small letters and steady pressure throughout.
(page 42)

HUMILITY is indicated in a somewhat modest way; there are two degrees of humility; there is the true self-respecting virtue and the slavish bowing down! But the first view of one's modesty is in the letter M. When we find each M of equal form, equal height and rather close together, we may safely pronounce the writer modest and rather shy in society. An unobtrusive writing is timid and retiring, small, sometimes with a leftward slant. Simplicity and absence of ostentation and flourish are noticeable.

IMAGINATION The imaginative writer lives in a dream world which you will easily recognise! First you will notice that the writing has a full appearance with emphasis on the upper loops.

The letters are long and the capitals are large and elegant. This writer hurries over work, the hand tries to catch the ideas and illegibility is sometimes the result. If to the partial illegibility we find a poetic or artistic taste in graceful and original capitals, we may rest assured that we have a hurried person, a writer who is fired by his brain and wishes to strike while the iron is hot! The quick writer, the man or woman of much novel-writing, is generally indistinct. The brain works quickly and the hand must follow. *(page 44)*

IMPATIENCE will be found associated with impulse and haste. The crossing of the t above the letter, or when hurriedly made, will naturally lead us to ascribe impatience and petulance to

had a lovely
thanks for your
it arived

Round letters of equal height
(Kindness)

our correspondent. The ways in which the stops are fashioned, not carefully rounded, but with small hooks, will tell us of an impatient temperament. The indications of will are not very strong in the really impatient hand, for a person who possesses self-control is not outwardly impatient.

IMPULSIVENESS is a sudden effort of mind resulting in certain 'flying' letters. Predominantly, there is a rightward slant, with no starting strokes to the letters. An impulsive writing will generally have a lively appearance about it, coupled with flying t-bars. *(page 44)*

INDECISION is shown in varying sizes of letters and words. Look for undulating writing without a steady

you for your letter
your lecture as
to seeing you

Large forward slanting script
(Leadership)

base line. This writing will have no sense of direction either. In an indecisive person you will find left, upright and rightward leaning letters, all in the same script! Another give-away is an absent or weak t-bar.

INDOLENCE is characterised by a softness of style. The writing will have no urgency about it, with rounded turns to the letters. In contrast, energy is seen in angular writing; indolence and laziness are shown by a kind of 'willing-to-be-amused' writing, as seen in soft, round, often upright letters. Someone who writes with a rounded, good-natured, but indolent hand, enjoys life in a quiet way without putting themselves out too much! *(page 46)*

INTELLIGENCE is one of the most difficult traits to recognise. There are no strict rules that will allow you to identify intelligence, but it is sometimes marked by a general harmony and elegance to the writing. Handwriting showing high intelligence is often small and illegible. There is a coolness and determination in the penmanship.

INTUITIVE traits are easily detected when the first and second letters of a word are not joined. When you find small gaps here and there throughout the script, you can be sure this person relies on intuition in their decision making.

for my soul. More
this world dreams of.
like a fountain for
what are men better

Connected letters and words
(Logic)

what you are
start to begin

Forward sloping, long ending strokes
(Love)

Proxy Park for the
for the most appea
- sounds like fun!

Closed a and o letters
(Loyalty)

Dear Emily

Small capital letters
(Modesty)

JEALOUSY is found in a very sloping hand, together with long-looped l, y and g. This is love and romantic regard. We must look for traces of egotism, imagination, tenderness and impulse. In addition to sloping writing and looped letters, you should also pay attention to the t-bar. A knotted t-bar can be a sign of persistence and jealousy. This person will possess a great imagination and build castles on a very slight foundation! *(page 46)*

JOCULAR This is a very pleasing trait in any handwriting and can be deduced from original letter forms. You will often find considerable eccentricity in the forms of the letters in the dry, witty person. The spirit of fun is very recognisable.

JUDGEMENT is another complicated attribute in graphology. A sign of good judgement is shown in upright writing, (the writer can see both sides of a problem) together with g and y strokes that go straight down, with no return loop.

KINDNESS is observable in rounded letters. We may find it associated with very tender writing, that is sloping writing, and also the more upright hand. The letters generally are of almost equal height, and their roundedness tell us of the kindly good-tempered hand. The kindness may arise from an easy-going temperament which is a passive kindliness; but your more active philanthropist will have the marks of energy in their writing. *(page 50)*

LAZINESS is a compound of indolence, idleness and indecision, so we must not expect to find any of the signs of energy in a lazy person! There is a carelessness about it, a difference in the sizes of letters and a softness in the rounded, rather large and somewhat upright writing. The writing will frequently drop downwards.

LEADERSHIP is indicated by the size of the writing. Leaders are confident and therefore write with a firm pressure. These people are capable of inspiring others and write with a large forward slanting script. Often the right

to do
to love &
to hope for

Decided crossing of the t
(Obstinacy)

margin will be absent, as these writers are not afraid to face a challenge. The signature is often larger than the rest of the script. *(page 52)*

LOGIC is shown by connected letters and words, revealing a continuity of thought. Reason and intelligence are strongly developed. Good speakers generally write hands in which logic, criticism and imagination are united.
(page 55)

LOVE Forward sloping writing is a good sign of the romantic. The warm-hearted will have a garland style, with harmonious rhythm. Look for full loops, a dominant middle zone and long ending strokes. *(page 55)*

Thought it was
a few lines. I'm afraid
for today, but if there
rather, I mean delivery —
should receive this then

Neat regular handwriting
(Minutiae)

LOYALTY will be indicated by firm, slightly ascending writing with roundness and gentleness. Clear letter forms and layout, in particular with closed o and a, confirming a discreet nature. *(page 56)*

MELANCHOLY Shown in a continued downward direction of the writing, frequently small, with light pressure. Left-directed letters will often be present showing a preoccupation with past events.

MINUTIAE A love of detail, can be seen in small, neat regular handwriting, of a rather upright character; the stops, dots and dashes, will all be carefully inserted in their proper places. *(page 62)*

Don't let anyone
Enjoy the 'booty'
Sail on through
& have many
discoveries on

Definite signs of care and attention
(Orderliness)

MISERLY persons will write a cramped hand; frequently small and close sparing of ink and paper; no generous curves and flourishes to the final letters. Of course prudence and economy are praiseworthy, but the sudden ending of words, coupled with the absence of any features of generosity are the salient points of the miserly individual! This writer has no sympathy with expenditure in any form, and will object to any unnecessary expense.

MODESTY is to be found in the sizes of the capital letters relative to the smaller ones. If we find small capital letters with an unadorned signature, we may decide that the writer is of an unpretentious and modest nature.
(page 56)

walk the dog
Park is another
usually somewhere

Stable base line
(Patience)

that after this
that the place

Long t-bars showing a firm decided mind
(Perseverance)

MUSICAL Music is the language of the soul, and likely to stir the feelings and imagination deeply! We find originality in musicians, so we should be on the look out for quaintness of capitals, eccentric letters also at times, but generally gracefulness and harmony are most evident. The letter 'd' can be formed like a musical note.

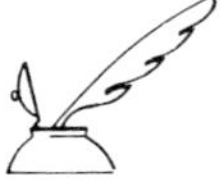

OBSTINACY Indications of the obstinate writer are similar to those of a stubborn one! The first thing to look

Things, but
them to
forget their
spoken they

Heavy pressure , angular script
(Quarrelsome)

for is firmness and decision in the writing, the decided crossing of the t particularly being characteristic, often with a heavy pressure too. *(page 60)*

OPTIMISM can be spotted easily by robust writing, soaring lines and a signature to match!

ORDERLINESS like minutiae, can be seen at a glance. Look for even, balanced writing, with all punctuation being in its rightful place! The t will be crossed carefully and the margins well defined. These definite signs of care and attention are all reliable pointers to an orderly mind. *(page 64)*

PATIENCE These people will write a hand in which no signs of irritability

This is also a title of my

A hurried appearance
(Quickness)

Please read

Leftward leaning compressed style.
(Reserve)

will be observable. Generally upright or slightly leftward slanting, but always with a stable baseline and rounded forms. *(page 66)*

PERSEVERANCE In a persevering handwriting there will be energy and rather long bars to the t - showing a firm, decided mind. Another giveaway, is the knotted t. The writing will be angular with heavy pressure and the letters within words are linked. *(page 66)*

PRIDE A haughty disdain for our fellow-creatures will be discovered in writing in which the capital letters are increased in size. An upright hand, with accentuated capital I and a signature with the initial of the middle name added can all be signs of pride. *(page 72)*

My grand
is buried in
complete with
a few yards
with roses

Upright hand with accentuated capitals
(Pride)

QUARRELSOME people write irregular and rather angular hands, but the clearest indication is very heavy pressure to the writing. Run your fingers over the back of the paper to feel the force of these individuals. The letter p can have a tall spike on the top. Another feature typical of the quarrelsome nature, is long starting strokes. *(page 68)*

QUICKNESS of thought has an energy in the writing and traces of versatility. The writing has a hurried appearance about it. T-bars and i-dots are dashed. In a quick-thinker, you will find a simplified script and pointed tops to the m and n. Words can disappear into a thread-like line.
(page 70)

Beat the egg yolks
apples into a pan
and sugar. Cover
apple mixture.

Greek E and backward curling d
(Refinement)

REFINEMENT is shown by graceful capital letters. There is no coarseness, nor thickness in the script. In refined individuals, you will see a wide left margin, often a Greek E and the letter d returns to the left showing a leaning toward literary taste. *(page 74)*

RESERVE in handwriting is discovered by the closing of the letter o and a, the lower parts of the d etc. No one of a self-contained and "ungushing" disposition ever keeps the loops open! There is always an upright or leftward leaning handwriting, coupled with a compressed style of letter-form is a good indication of reserve. *(page 70)*

live as long
want as long

Full g and y loops
(Romantic)

woman, loving, patient
blessing in our
brave to bear the

Leftward leaning arcade style
(Secretive)

ROMANTIC A person who looks on the romantic side of life, will have long full g and y loops, flourishes to their word endings and highly developed upper zones. The dreamy character will frequently doodle rounded unaggressive shapes, such as daisies and hearts. *(page 76)*

SECRETIVE persons will knot their letters a and o at the top. The arcade style handwriting will be compressed, sometimes with a leftward leaning script. A wide margin all around is a good indicator of a secretive person. The signature can be enclosed in a circular movement; keeping people at arm's length! *(page 76)*

entitled
ference dinner
Museum.

Added loop to t and d
(Sensitive)

We have

been a long

Generous spacing between lines and words
(Self-contained)

SELF-CONTAINED people close up their letters. There will be generous spacing between the lines and words, denoting no particular need for company. Small, upright writing will be found in self-contained persons. *(page 78)*

SENSITIVITY is indicated by writing that is extremely light in pressure. Such people are frequently "touchy" and apt to think themselves slighted when there is really no reason for their fears. Sensitivity is also revealed by the letter d, which will have an added loop to the stem. *(page 78)*

SENSUALITY The writing will be dominated by thick pressure on the lower loops which will be rounded and full. The overall impression will be

Creep home
The spent
God grant
You loved

Emphasis on lower loops
(Sensuality)

unrestricted and free with a particular emphasis on broad letter forms. *(page 80)*

SENTIMENTAL individuals will write with a forward slant, with long endings to their words, the garland style will predominate throughout. These writers will use all the paper available to them with a larger than average middle zone. *(page 82)*

SPONTANEITY is found in the imaginative hand, with rather flying crosses to the t-bar, and movement in the writing, the letters perhaps being of different heights. This presupposes a certain versatility of mind and rapid change of thought. There will be an absence of starting strokes. *(page 82)*

For the one eye
The moments'

Garland style predominates
(Sentimental)

money. What
handwriting
have been to

Absence of starting strokes
(Spontaneity)

STUBBORNNESS will be seen in strong writing. This characteristic is revealed by a heavy writing and elongated final strokes. The letters m and n have endings which plunge downwards.

TACT is revealed by straight base lines, a small to medium size, with letters getting smaller towards the end of the words. The letters a and o will be firmly closed. *(page 84)*

TALKATIVE people reveal themselves by words spaced closely together; the letter a and o will be open at the top. Broad letters and rising lines are sure signs of a talkative person! A talkative person who can nevertheless be trusted will display this style but with closed a and o letters.

garden in autumn
rusts and golds
the bare branches
The spring comes
bright red tulips.

Words decreasing in size
(Tact)

TEMPER is shown in angular letters and in the hasty flying bars to the letter t. The pressure will be very heavy, the writing irregular, coupled with an uneven base line. Hooks may also be added to letters. *(page 86)*

TENACITY The long thick stroke to the small t bar, will give us tenacity, determined and firm, angular, indicating force. Look for clear spacing, speed and an upward hook on the right of the t bar, coupled with an ascending appearance. *(page 86)*

TENDERNESS To find tenderness we must look for signs in sloping writing and kindly curves. There will be no aggressive tendencies in this handwriting.

any faith in
cleared thine

Extreme heavy pressure, hooks added
(Temper)

through the
relaxing, I

Upward hook to t-bar
(Tenacity)

THRIFT is judged by the same standard as economy. The words stop short, and no more expenditure of ink than is necessary is evident.

TRUTHFULNESS Truth has no fear, no wish to conceal anything and, consequently, the perfectly truthful candid person writes a perfectly clear open hand! The letters are nearly always of the same size, with even lines and spacing. The really untruthful person who wishes to swindle you writes a (purposely) indistinct hand. The writer who runs letters into a line with the pen (thread connection) creates unformed letters and indicates the wish to conceal something! *(page 88)*

if you
goes uphill –
paper. Also,
names on ca
are different
example:

Clear, open hand
(Truthfulness)

Dear Linda:

LETTER~BOX

Ornamentation to letter L and R (Vanity)

with lemon
for sweet
I enjoyed

Different heights and sizes of letters (Versatility)

dearly like to
another kind
with you. but at
must decline
we will
touch. and

Strong straight strokes
(Will)

VANITY This little human trait is most evident in a flourish beneath the signature. As a rule, much flourish may be accepted as an indication of egotism and vulgarity. Also capital letters written with much ornamentation are a sign of vanity, particularly capital L and R. *(page 89)*

VERSATILITY is accentuated by the different heights and sizes of letters with rounded curves at the ends. There is also some inconsistency in such writing, variation in t-bar placing and letters in general. *(page 89)*

VIVACITY is indicated by ascending words, quick rhythmic writing with no unnecessary breaks or amendments. We can all recognise the vivacious person;

I reget that
my new role
formally hand-over

Amended strokes
(Worry)

the writing has a feeling of liveliness about it. It is also executed with some pressure, revealing high levels of energy.

VULGARITY may be measured by the forms of the capitals which, if ungraceful with a vulgar flourish, indicate a want of cultivation. This large writing is an attempt to be showy and all such display, whether it take the form of 'loud' garments, profusion of jewellery or writing is vulgar!

WEAKNESS Bodily weakness is shown in the descending character of the writing, throughout the page. Another sign is a carelessness and want of force. The pressure will be light and the style undisciplined.

WILL is perceptible in an almost infinite number of signs and shades, from the cruel to the gentle.

We can all judge from our own writing, whether or not we are obstinate, arbitrary or yielding.

The despot drives the pen with an iron will across the letter, and holds it firmly at the end.

Will is accentuated also when the y and g have no return tails, and end in strong straight strokes at the end. These signs are often and nearly always accompanied by a single line beneath the signature, sometimes a very thick line.

When the t is crossed high, with flying strokes, we have energy and irritability of temper. A thin stroke or no cross at all on the t indicates absence of willpower. A reference to the other characteristics will soon confirm or modify our first impressions. *(page 90)*

WORRY will display itself as a despondent and rather irritable hand. Sometimes the traces of worry are very apparent *(see signatures page 103)*, but a great deal will depend upon the will-power of the individual. Of course, a strong-willed person will endeavour to triumph over their difficulties, and then the signs of worry will virtually be obliterated. However, occasionally we shall find the traces of trouble and anxiety in uncertain letter forms and amended strokes. *(page 92)*

CONTRASTS AND GENERALITIES

By now you will have learned that graphology is not just a case of looking for one letter or another, one loop or another. In every hand we must be prepared to find contradictions and opposing tendencies. There are some useful factors which will help you to practise your graphology on letters you receive, notes colleagues leave for you, etc. We begin with the four script styles: garland, arcade, thread and angular.

Analyse a piece of writing, preferably no more than 6 months old, and decide which of the following script formations it most closely matches:

Garland Style

People who write in a garland style are usually kind hearted and affectionate. They will often have a spontaneous, receptive nature but can be easily influenced. These people are more likely to be followers than leaders. A person with this style of writing dislikes conflict.

Arcade Style

A person who writes with an arcade style is usually trustworthy and diplomatic. They will be the more reserved ones in a crowd and have to be careful not to become emotionally isolated, as they tend to keep their feelings hidden. These are proud, independent people.

Thread Style

Instinctive and creative are the best two words to describe writers with this style. These people are mentally alert and keep all options firmly open although they can be evasive. They can be rebels too!

Angular Style

Planners and organisers write in an angular style. They are conscientious and strong minded but can sometimes be irritable and uncompromising. These people want to be in control.

Signatures

Your signature is unique - it reveals how you like to be seen by others and is obviously the most frequent example of handwriting.

The signature is a written self-portrait and when seen together with other aspects of your writing will reveal various intriguing facets of your personality. In graphology, the signature is seen as the symbol of the ego.

When carrying out an in-depth report, you need a sample of the writer's natural handwriting plus the signature, which can sometimes be quite different

compared to the main body of the text. The main body will reveal the writer's intellectual, emotional and sexual makeup, but the signature will show the outer image - that which they wish to portray to the world.
Once it is formed, the structure of the signature remains the same, but can alter due to outside influences such as emotional problems, ill-health and of course, old-age.
However, while a signature by itself is not conclusive enough for a full graphological report, much can be deduced from it.

Look out for these signature styles as you read character in handwriting...

Complicated

Indicates the pretentious writer, possibly lacking in a sense of proportion.

Width

Width - particularly those who execute in a wide and expansive movement, (especially if large as well), will indicate that the writer wants elbow room as well as a platform to display his ego.

Underlining

With an underlining, downward stroke not joined to the name - strong but cautious nature.

With an underlining, rising stroke - great strength of will and self-esteem.

Ascending

A sign of ambition, good humour.

Simple

Absence of any flourish - modesty, self-confidence.

Endings

Signature followed by:

a downward stroke joined to the last letter - resolution, possibly someone to quickly take offence.

a surrounding stroke, framing the name - secretiveness, wariness, a great amount of self-protectiveness.

a dot - prudence, self-consciousness; a liking to have the final word!

Further Acknowledgements

Original Victorian publication 'How to Read Character in Handwriting' by Henry Frith published 1890.

Additional editorial for this edition, Nat Barnes.

The compiler and publishers would like to thank all those people who have allowed their handwriting to be published as examples.

If you have enjoyed this Copper Beech Gift Book, you may also enjoy:

The Ladies Oracle

Life's questions answered.
Shall I soon be courted?
May I hope to receive a fortune?
The answers to these and other questions may be found by consulting this oracle devised in 1857.

A Garter Round The Bedpost

Love charms and superstitions collected from the 18th and 19th centuries.
As well as garters (twine one nine times round the bedpost to dream of your future love), there's advice about come-hither dressing:
'Those dressed in blue/Have lovers true...'

For your free catalogue write to
Copper Beech Publishing Ltd
P O Box 159, East Grinstead, Sussex RH19 4FS
England

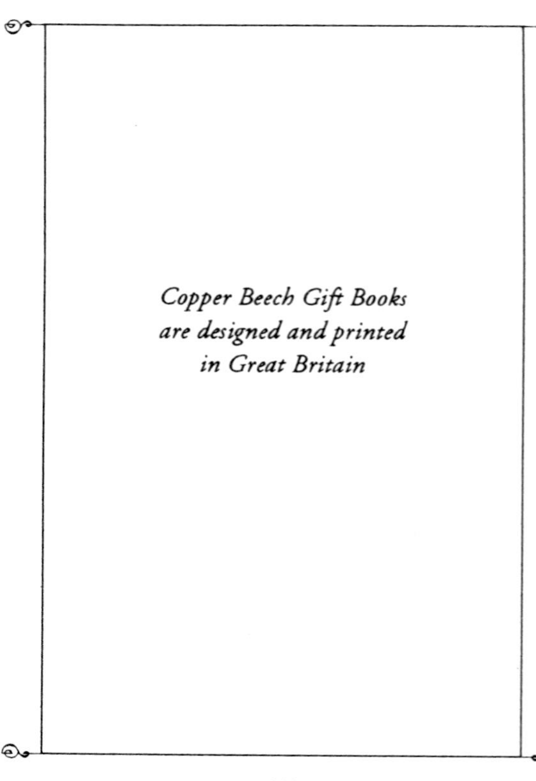

Copper Beech Gift Books
are designed and printed
in Great Britain